The British Pie Week Cookbook: Recipes to Enjoy for Days

Perfect Pie You Want to Try At Home

Table of Contents

Introduction 4

Savory 7

  1. Curried Beef Pie 8

  2. Lamb Shanks Pie 12

  3. Steak and Kidney Pie............................17

  4. Squab Pie 21

  5. Sweeney Todd's Meat Pies...................25

  6. Bedfordshire Clanger.............................30

  7. Lancashire Butter Pie............................34

  8. Welsh Leek and Ham Pie 38

  9. Steak and Stilton Pies 41

  10. Lord Woolton Pie 45

  11. Cauliflower Cheese Pie........................49

  12. Forfar Bridies......................................53

  13. Scotch Pies..57

  14. Chicken, Leek, Prune and Caerphilly Pie 61

  15. Stargazey Pie 65

  16. Cheshire Pork Pie 69

  17. Homity Pie...72

  18. Corned Beef Pie..................................75

  19. Game Pie..79

20. Country Style Tomato Pie 83

21. Fish, Chip, and Mushy Pea Pie.........................86

22. Gala Pie...89

23. Coronation Chicken Pie..............................94

24. Katt Pie 98

25. Smoked Fish Pie in Shortcrust Pastry................101

Sweet...*104*

26. Nutmeg Spiced Custard Tarts........................105

27. Lemon Meringue Pie 109

28. Plum, Apple, and Sloe Gin Pie 112

29. Banoffee Pie.......................................115

30. Manchester Tart 117

31. Mini Jam Jewel Tarts..............................120

32. Apple and Blackberry Pie 123

33. Mince Pie 127

34. Gypsy Tart 130

35. Bakewell Tart......................................132

36. Bilberry Lattice Pie...............................136

37. Maids of Honour Pies 139

Introduction

That the Brits love pies is an understatement of the century. We can see that in the number of pies available in the country.

There are over 40 types of pies in Britain. Talking about the apple pie, black bun pie, bacon and egg pie, chicken and mushroom pie, butter pie, devizes pie, gypsy pie, humble pie, maids of honour tart, meat, and potato pie, etc., you can't but agree that pies are as to the Brits what beer/sausage is to the Germans!

Another reason why pies are known as Pastry for the Brits is the British Pie Week. Who hosts an entire country to a feast of pies? No other country does this except the Brits!

The British Pie Week is a week-long event where everyone comes to showcase their pies!

In that event, you would see and eat as many pies as possible. You would see pies that you never thought existed!

Having attended a couple of these events, I got introduced to a couple of pie types, and I was blown away.

And I had no choice than to compile them in this recipe book for you to enjoy and try out in your home!

If you have craving to have a pie fest in your home just like the British Pie Week, then this recipe book is your best shot!

In this recipe book, you would find different pie recipes that you can entertain your guests with!!!

Turn the page and let's get baking!!!

Savory

1. Curried Beef Pie

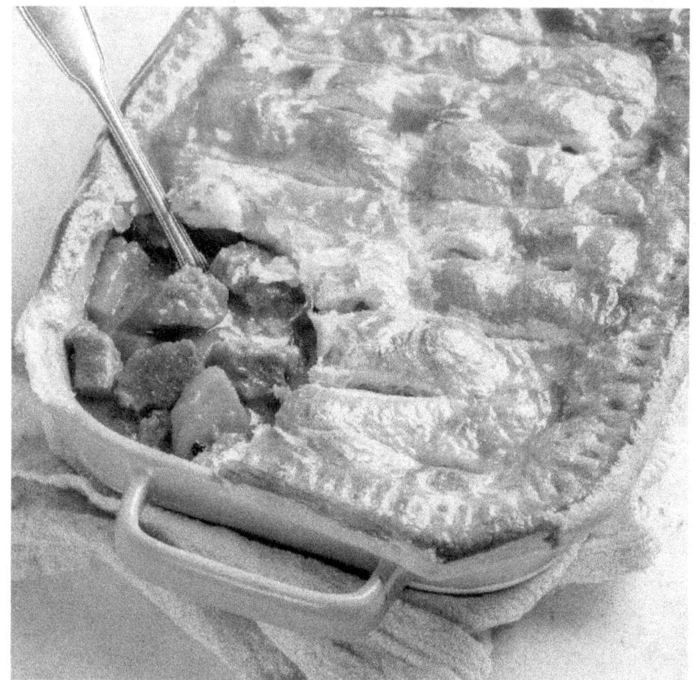

Servings: 6

Prep Time: 30 mins

Cooking Time: 3 hours 30 mins

Total Time: 4 hours

The list of ingredients:

- 2 tbsp. brown sugar

- Water

- 1 (14 ounce) tin crushed tomatoes

- 3 sheets puff pastry

- 3 sheets shortcrust pastry, ready-made

- 2 cups beef stock

- 1/2 cup plain flour

- 3 brown onions (peeled, chopped)

- 1/4 tsp. ground white pepper

- 3 cloves garlic (peeled, chopped)

- 1/4 cup vegetable oil

- 1 medium egg (lightly beaten)

- 1/4 cup curry powder

- 2½ pounds shin beef (cut into ¾"cubes)

- 1/2 tsp. salt

Method:

Step 1

Preheat the main oven to 360 degrees F.

Step 2

Cut the sheets of pastry in half diagonally and line 6 individual pie dishes with pastry. Trim the pastry's edges. Line the pie dishes with parchment paper and fill with baking beans. Bake on a baking tray for 25 minutes. Remove the beans and set aside to cool on a wire baking rack.

Step 3

Turn the oven temperature down to 280 degrees F.

Step 4

In a bowl, combine the flour with the salt, curry powder, white pepper, and meat. Toss to combine.

Step 5

In a large pan, over high heat, heat 1 tbsp of vegetable oil. Shake off any excess flour from the cubes of meat and brown a third of the meat on all sides. Set aside in a bowl. Repeat the process until all the meat has been browned.

Step 6

Reduce the temperature to moderate heat and add the remaining oil. Sauté the onions along with the garlic until softened but not browned.

Step 7

Return the meat to the pan, and add the crushed tomatoes along with the stock and brown sugar. Cover with a lid and transfer to the oven, until the meat is tender, this will take around 2 hours. If you feel the sauce needs to be thicker, remove the lid for the final 30 minutes of cooking.

Step 8

Allow to cool before you begin to fill the pies.

Step 9

Using the beaten egg, lightly brush the edges of the shortcrust pastry.

Step 10

Arrange the puff pastry over the top and gently, but firmly press around the rim to seal. Trim away excess pastry.

Step 11

Make a few slits in the top of the pie and brush with beaten egg along with 1 tbsp water.

Step 12

Increase the oven temperature to 400 degrees F.,

Step 13

Transfer to the oven until golden and puffed, this will take around 20-25 minutes.

2. Lamb Shanks Pie

Servings: 4

Prep Time: 30mins

Cooking Time: 2 hours 30 mins

Total Time: 3 hours

The list of ingredients:

- Salt

- 1¼ pints chicken stock
- 4 lamb shanks
- 1 pound 5 ounces potatoes (peeled, cut into 1" pieces)
- 1 tbsp rapeseed oil
- 10½ ounces cooked peas (prepared, optional)
- 2 onions (peeled, roughly chopped)
- 2 sprigs fresh rosemary
- 4 garlic cloves (peeled, crushed)
- 9 ounces white wine
- 4 sprigs fresh thyme
- Salt and freshly ground black pepper
- 1 medium egg
- 14 ounces ready-made puff pastry
- 3 large carrots (cut into 1" pieces)
- 2 tbsp plain flour + additional for dusting
- 1 (14 ounce) tin haricot beans (drained)
- 2 bay leaves
- Mashed potato (prepared, optional)
- 1 medium egg yolk (lightly beaten)
- 4 celery stalks (cut into 1" pieces)

Method:

Step 1

Preheat the main oven to 340 degrees F.

Step 2

Generously season the lamb with salt and pepper.

Step 3

In a flame-proof and ovenproof, large casserole dish, over high heat, heat the rapeseed oil.

Step 4

Add the shanks of lamb and fry on all sides for a few seconds, until browned evenly all over. Remove from the dish and put to one side.

Step 5

Turn the heat down to moderate, add the onions and sauté for 2-3 minutes, or until just softened.

Step 6

Add the garlic and fry for a couple of minutes before stirring in the flour so that it forms a paste when combined with the juices in the pan. Continue to cook for 60 seconds.

Step 7

Pour in the wine followed by the stock and stir to incorporate it into the flour mixture.

Step 8

Add the pieces of potato along with the carrots, celery, bay leaves, thyme, and rosemary and bring to boil. Turn the heat down to a simmer.

Step 9

Add the drained beans.

Step 10

Return the lamb to the dish and bring back to a simmer. Cover the dish with a tight-fitting lid and transfer to the preheated oven for 2 hours, or until the meat falls easily off the bone.

Step 11

Remove the dish from the oven and transfer the mixture to a pie dish. Arrange the shanks of lamb so that they are upright.

Step 12

Set to one side to completely cool.

Step 13

Preheat the oven to 360 degrees F.

Step 14

Lightly brush the outside and the inside rims of the pie dish with a little beaten egg and yolk.

Step 15

Roll the pastry out onto a lightly floured, clean worktop until it is approximately 2" larger than the diameter of the pie dish and approximately ¼" thick.

Step 16

Lay the pastry over the lamb in the dish.

Step 17

Take a sharp bladed knife and make 4 small slits in the pastry next to the lamb bones, and gently form the pastry around the bones, to ensure that they stick through.

Step 18

Crimp the pastry around the edge of the dish to seal it and lightly brush with the remaining egg. Scatter the surface of the pie, with a little salt.

Step 19

Serve with peas and mashed potato.

3. Steak and Kidney Pie

Servings: 6

Prep Time: 20 mins

Cooking Time: 50 mins

Total Time: 1 hour 10 mins

The list of ingredients:

- Pepper

- 3 tbsp. unsalted butter

- Salt

- 1½ pounds beef tenderloin

- 1 celery stalk (trimmed, chopped)

- 2 tbsp. canola oil

- 2 tbsp. all-purpose flour

- 1 (11 ounce) puff pastry sheet

- 1 carrot (chopped)

- 2 cups beef stock

- 3/4 pound lamb kidneys

- 1 shallot (chopped)

- 1 tsp. fresh thyme

Method:

Step 1

Preheat the main oven to 400 degrees F. using parchment paper, line a large baking sheet.

Step 2

Cut the pastry into 6 disks, and arrange them in a single layer, not touching one another, on the baking sheet.

Step 3

Bake in the upper third of the main oven for 5-7 minutes, or until golden brown. Set to one side to cool on a wire baking rack.

Step 4

Season the beef and lamb kidneys.

Step 5

In a skillet or frying pan over moderately high heat, heat the oil.

Step 6

Working in batches of 3 or 4, sauté the meat, while occasionally turning, until just browned.

Step 7

Cook each batch of meat for between 5-8 minutes.

Step 8

Take out of the pan with a slotted spoon and put to one side.

Step 9

Turn the heat down to moderate; add the shallot, carrot, and celery to the pan and fry until the veggies are fork tender, frequently stirring for 5-6 minutes.

Step 10

Add the flour to the pan and cook, while constantly stirring for 60 seconds.

Step 11

Return the meat to the pan, and a little at a time stir in the beef stock.

Step 12

Bring to boil, frequently stirring and add the butter. Stir to combine and season. Add the thyme and stir.

Step 13

When you are ready to serve, divide the meat mixture between 6 bowls and top each one with a golden puff pastry disk.

4. Squab Pie

Servings: 4

Prep Time: 15 mins

Cooking Time: 1 hour 15 mins

Total Time: 1 hour 30 mins

The list of ingredients:

- 3 level tbsp cornflour

- 1 pound ready to roll shortcrust pastry

- 1 medium egg (beaten, to glaze)

- 1 tsp. soft brown sugar

- 1 large Granny Smith apple (peeled, cored, thinly sliced)

- 1 pound lamb steaks (cut into bite-sized pieces)

- 1 tsp. mixed spice

- 1 red onion (peeled, halved, thinly sliced)

- 1 ¾ cups cold lamb stock

- Floor (for rolling)

Method:

Step 1

Preheat the main oven to 400 degrees F.

Step 2

In a bowl, combine the cornflour with the mixed spice and sugar.

Step 3

Add the lamb pieces and toss to combine.

Step 4

In a 10" pie dish, layer the meat, with the red onion and apple.

Step 5

Sprinkle the leftover cornflour mixture over the meat mixture and pour in the stock.

Step 6

On a lightly floured, clean worktop, roll out the ready-made pastry to the thickness of ⅛".

Step 7

Cut out a lid sufficiently large enough to cover the pie dish together with a long strip to go around the edge.

Step 8

Wet the edge of the pie dish and press on the pastry strip.

Step 9

Cover with the pastry lid and seal and crimp the edges.

Step 10

Make 2 slits in the top of the pie, as this will allow the steam to escape.

Step 11

Lightly brush the pie with egg and cook in the oven for between 12-15 minutes, until the pastry begins to brown.

Step 12

Reduce the heat to 320 degrees F and cook for 60
minutes.

Step 13

If the pastry begins to brown too quickly loosely
tent with aluminum foil.

5. Sweeney Todd's Meat Pies

Servings: 10

Prep Time: 40 mins

Cooking Time: 15 mins

Total Time: 55 mins

The list of ingredients:

Pastry:

- 1¼ cups cold butter
- 10½ ounces plain flour
- Cold water
- Pinch of salt

Filling:

- 1 pound minced beef
- 1/2 cup beef stock
- 1/2 tsp. celery salt
- 1 tbsp. Worcestershire sauce
- 3 tbsp. tomato puree
- 2 tbsp oil
- 1 tbsp. tomato ketchup
- 1 medium egg (beaten, to glaze)
- 1 large onion (peeled, finely diced)
- 1 tbsp. plain flour
- Salt and pepper

Method:

Step 1

First, make the pastry.

Step 2

Add the flour to a large mixing bowl along with a
pinch of salt and stir to combine.

Step 3

Add the cold butter and using clean fingertips rub
together until you achieve a breadcrumb
consistency.

Step 4

In the middle make a well, 1 tablespoon at a time,
add cold water, until the mixture forms a dough.
Cover with plastic wrap and transfer to the
refrigerator for half an hour.

Step 5

Preheat the main oven to 390 degrees F and lightly
grease a muffin tray.

Step 6

In the meantime, make the filling by heating the oil
in a pan, and adding the onions along with the
minced beef, cook over moderately high heat, until
browned, 5 minutes.

Step 7

Add the puree, celery salt, ketchup and Worcestershire sauce. Stir to combine and season.

Step 8

In another bowl, a little at a time, whisk the beef stock into the tablespoon of plain flour until lump free and incorporated. Add to the meat and bring to the boil, cooking for a few minutes, until just thickened. Remove the pan from the heat.

Step 9

On a clean, lightly floured worktop roll out the pastry.

Step 10

Using a circular cutter, a little larger than the muffin trays circumference, cut out 10 circles and arrange them in the tray.

Step 11

Evenly distribute the meat filling between the muffin cups and using the remaining scraps and trimmings roll out, and cut 10 pie tops.

Step 12

Brush the pie rims with beaten eggs, arrange the tops on and gently seal.

Step 13

Take a sharp knife and make a couple of slits on each pie, to allow the steam to escape easily.

Step 14

Brush the tops of the pies with the remaining egg wash.

Step 15

Bake until golden brown, this will take around 15 minutes.

6. Bedfordshire Clanger

Servings: 9

Prep Time: 15 mins

Cooking Time: 45 mins

Total Time: 2 hours

The list of ingredients:

Filling:

- salt and pepper
- 2 granny smith apples (cored, peeled, diced)
- 13 ounces apricot jam
- 1 cup apple cider
- oil
- 16 ounces roast pork (chopped into small cubes)
- 1 yellow onion (peeled, diced)

Pastry:

- 1 egg
- 16 ounces plain flour + additional for dusting
- 1/2-3/4 cup ice water
- 1½ tsp. salt
- 5 ounces suet
- 1 egg (beaten, to use as egg wash)
- 1/3 cup salted butter (chilled, cubed)

Method:

Step 1

First, make the filling. In a pan sauté the onion in 1-2 tbsp of oil.

Step 2

Add the apples and pour in the cider and cook until the apples become soft. Add the cubed pork and season. Set to one side to completely cool.

Step 3

Next, make the pastry. Add the suet together with the butter to a food processor and blitz until small pieces are formed. Add the flour together with the salt and 1 egg, pulse until the mixture comes together, adding sufficient ice water as necessary.

Step 4

Shape the mixture into 3 equal balls and cover in kitchen wrap before transferring to the refrigerator for 60 minutes.

Step 5

Preheat the main oven to 440 degrees F. Using parchment paper, line 3 baking trays.

Step 6

Roll out 1 of the dough balls. The dough needs to be thin without breaking.

Step 7

Trim around the edges to make a rectangle and equally divide the dough into 3 pieces, using a sharp knife.

Step 8

Fill the center with the pork, around ¾ of the way down, adding a heaped tbsp of your preferred jam at the bottom.

Step 9

Brush the pastry around the edges with the egg wash. Roll and seal.

Step 10

Transfer the pie to a tray and arrange seam-side facing down. Repeat the process with the remaining pastry, remembering to brush with the egg.

Step 11

Bake in the oven for 15 minutes before reducing the heat to 380 degrees F and baking for a further 15 minutes.

Step 12

Serve.

7. Lancashire Butter Pie

Servings: 6

Prep Time: 30 mins

Cooking Time: 1 hour

Total Time: 1 hour 30 mins

The list of ingredients:

- 1 medium egg (whisked)

- 5 large potatoes (peeled, thinly sliced)

- 3 ounces butter

- 11 ounces shortcrust pastry, ready rolled (room temperature)

- 2 large onions (peeled, sliced)

- 11 ounces puff pastry sheet, ready rolled (room temperature)

Method:

Step 1

In a pan of boiling salty water, parboil the potatoes for 5 minutes. Drain.

Step 2

In a frying pan, over moderate heat, sauté the onions in butter until softened.

Step 3

Add the potatoes and stir to combine.

Step 4

In the meantime, and while the potato mixture is cooling, preheat the main oven to 400 degrees F.

Step 5

Lightly grease a 12" pie dish.

Step 6

Line the dish with the shortcrust pastry. Trim the
edges.

Step 7

Line with parchment paper and add baking beans.

Step 8

Bake in the oven, blind for 10 minutes.

Step 9

Remove the dish from the oven and allow to cool
slightly. Take the baking beans out of the dish.

Step 10

Set the oven to 425 degrees F.

Step 11

Add the potato filling to the pie shell and spread
evenly.

Step 12

Lay the puff pastry over the filling and crimp the
edges.

Step 13

Make slits in the top of the pie to allow the steam to
escape.

Step 14

Brush the pie with whisked egg and bake in the
oven for 15 minutes, or until golden.

Step 15

    Serve.

8. Welsh Leek and Ham Pie

Servings: 6

Prep Time: 10mins

Cooking Time: 45 mins

Total Time: 55 mins

The list of ingredients:

- 2½ cups single cream

- 8 ounces leeks

- Salt and pepper

- 2 ounces butter

- Milk (to glaze)

- 2 medium eggs

- 14 ounces ready-made pastry for double-crust pie

- 4 ounces boiled ham (chopped small)

Method:

Step 1

First, prepare the leeks. Cut off the roots along with any damaged parts of the outer layer and coarse green leaves. Under cold running tap water rinse the leeks to get rid of any grit and dirt.

Step 2

Slice the leeks into a colander and rinse once more.

Step 3

In a pan, melt the butter and cook the leeks, until fork tender.

Step 4

Line a shallow pie dish with a layer of pastry and add the leeks along with the boiled ham.

Step 5

In a bowl, combine the cream with the eggs and mix until incorporated. Season with salt and pepper and carefully strain into the pie dish. Cover the filling with a pastry lid and lightly brush with milk.

Step 6

Bake in the oven at 350 degrees F for half an hour.

Step 7

Enjoy warm rather than hot.

9. Steak and Stilton Pies

Servings: 4 individual pies

Prep Time: 25 mins

Cooking Time: 3 hours 10 mins

Total Time: 3 hours 35 mins

The list of ingredients:

- 10 ounces mushrooms (peeled, quartered)

- 10 ounces frozen peas

- 1 tbsp. unsalted butter

- 2 cups beef stock

- 2 garlic cloves (chopped finely)

- 2 tbsp rosemary (minced)

- 1 medium egg (beaten)

- 2 tsp. mustard powder

- 1 (12 ounce) bottle stout beer

- 14 ounces ready-made chilled puff pastry

- 1/4 cup olive oil

- 1 bay leaf

- 2 onions (peeled, sliced)

- 6 ounces English Stilton (crumbled)

- 2 carrots (peeled, sliced thickly)

- 2 stalks celery (sliced thickly)

- 1¼ pounds beef chuck (chopped into 1" cubes)

- 1/4 cup flour

Method:

Step 1

Over moderately high heat, heat the oil in a large pan.

Step 2

Season the beef cubes and cook for 10 minutes, until browned all over. When sufficiently cooked, transfer the beef to a mixing bowl.

Step 3

Add the garlic followed by the celery, onions, carrots, and rosemary and cook for just over 10 minutes.

Step 4

Pour in the beer, and cook until nearly dry, for 15-20 minutes.

Step 5

Add the flour and cook, while stirring, until silky smooth.

Step 6

Return the beef to the pan along with the beef stock, mustard powder and bay leaf; bring to a simmer over moderately low heat.

Step 7

Cook, while partially covered until the beef is just tender, this will take around 1½ hours. Set to one side.

Step 8

In a 10" frying pan over high heat, heat the butter.

Step 9

Add the quartered mushrooms and cook, while stirring, until browned all over, for 7-8 minutes. Stir into the beef mixture along with the crumbled cheese and frozen peas.

Step 10

Heat the oven to 375 degrees F.

Step 11

Evenly divide the filling between 4 (6") pie tins of approximately 12 ounces each.

Step 12

Roll the pastry out into 4 (6") circles.

Step 13

Brush the edges of the pie tins with beaten egg and position 1 circle over each, to seal.

Step 14

Cut slits into the pastry and lightly brush with beaten egg.

Step 15

Bake in the oven until browned, this will take around 35-40 minutes.

10. Lord Woolton Pie

Servings: 8

Prep Time: 30 mins

Cooking Time: 1 hour 30 mins

Total Time: 2 hours

The list of ingredients:

Filling:

- Bunch scallions (chopped)
- 1 tbsp. rolled oats
- 1 pound cauliflower (chopped into bite-size chunks)
- Salt and pepper
- 1 pound carrots (chopped into chunks)
- Fresh parsley
- 1 pound parsnips (chopped into bite-size chunks)
- 2 tsp. yeast extract paste
- 1 pound potatoes (peeled, chopped into bite-size chunks)

Pastry:

- 3 ounces margarine
- Milk
- Salt
- 4 ounces potato (mashed)
- 8 ounces whole meal flour
- Dash of water (optional)
- 2 tsp baking powder

Method:

Step 1

Add the cauliflower, parsnips, carrots, and potatoes in a large pot. Pour in just enough water to cover the veggies ¾ of the way, bring to simmer.

Step 2

Add the scallions, and yeast extract followed by the rolled oats, and add a dash of salt and pepper. Cook until the veggies are fork-tender and most of the water absorbed.

Step 3

Transfer the mixture to a deep pie dish and scatter with fresh parsley.

Step 4

Next, prepare the pastry. In a bowl, mixing the wholemeal flour with the baking powder and a pinch of salt and rub in the margarine.

Step 5

Add the mashed potato in to form a dough and knead. You can at this stage add a drop of water if the mixture is a little dry.

Step 6

Roll out to make a pie crust and arrange it on top of the filling. Brush with milk.

Step 7

Bake in the oven at 400 degrees F, for half an hour
or until the top is rim and golden brown.

11. Cauliflower Cheese Pie

Servings: 6

Prep Time: 15 mins

Cooking Times: 40 mins

Total Time: 55 mins

The list of ingredients:

- 1/2 cup plain flour

- 1 tsp. fresh nutmeg

- 3⅓ cups semi skim milk

- 2 tsp. English mustard

- 1 large cauliflower (cut into florets)

- 7 ounces mature cheddar cheese

- salt and pepper

- 3 cloves

- 1 (13ounce) package ready-made puff pastry

- 1 bay leaf

- 1/4 cup butter

- 1 medium egg (beaten)

- 1/2 yellow onion

Method:

Step 1

Preheat the main oven to 400 degrees F.

Step 2

Add the milk to a large pan along with the onion, cloves, nutmeg and bay leaf and bring to a simmer.

Step 3

Take the pan off the heat and put to one side for 10 minutes, this will allow the flavors to infuse.

Step 4

Strain, discard the onion along with the bay leaf and cloves.

Step 5

In a large pan, melt the butter and over moderate heat, add the flour, stir and cook for 2 minutes.

Step 6

Take the pan off the heat, and a little at a time, add the infused milk, while constantly stirring to ensure the mixture is lump free.

Step 7

Return the pan to the stove, and over moderate heat bring to the boil until thickened; this will take around 4-5 minutes.

Step 8

Add the cheese together with the mustard and seasoning.

Step 9

In a large pan of boiling water add the cauliflower, and cook until fork tender; 3-5 minutes.

Step 10

Drain the cauliflower and combine with the cheese sauce, stirring to incorporate.

Step 11

Transfer to a baking dish and arrange the puff
pastry on top, trimming off excess pastry from the
edges.

Step 12

Glaze generously with beaten egg and make a few
holes in the center of the pastry to allow the steam
to escape.

Step 13

Bake in the oven for between 25-30 minutes, or
until golden.

Step 14

Put to one side for several minutes before serving.

12. Forfar Bridies

Servings: 6 individual pies

Prep Time: 20 mins

Cooking Time: 1 hour 10 mins

Total Time: 1 hour 30 mins

The list of ingredients:

- 2 ounces butter

- 1 tsp dry mustard powder
- Cold water
- 2 onions (peeled, finely chopped)
- 1½ pounds lean, boneless rump steak (fat removed, pounded, cut into ½" pieces)
- Flour
- 1½ pounds ready-made shortcrust pastry
- Salt and black pepper
- Oil
- 1/4 cup rich beef stock

Method:

Step 1

Preheat the main oven to 450 degrees F.

Step 2

Add the pieces of steak to a bowl. Season with salt and pepper and add the mustard powder, onion, and butter along with the beef stock and mix to combine.

Step 3

Prepare the ready-made pastry according to the manufacturer's instructions and divide the meat and pastry into 6 equal-sized portions.

Step 4

On a lightly floured, clean work surface roll each of the 6 pastry portions into a circle of approximately 6" in diameter and no less than ¼" thickness.

Step 5

Spoon a portion of the meat mixture in the center of each circle, allowing an edge of pastry clear all around.

Step 6

Brush half of the pastry circle's outer edge with a drop of cold water and fold over. Using a fork, crimp the edges to seal.

Step 7

Make a small slit in the top of each pie, to allow the steam to escape.

Step 8

Brush a baking sheet with oil and arrange the bridies on the sheet in a single layer, and without touching one another.

Step 9

Transfer to the oven and bake for 15 minutes, before turning the heat down to 350 degrees F and cooking for a further 45-55 minutes.

Step 10

The pies are ready when they are golden brown. If during the baking process you feel they are getting too dark, too quickly, cover with foil.

Step 11

Serve.

13. Scotch Pies

Servings: 8

Prep Time: 30 mins

Cooking Time: 45 mins

Total Time: 1 hour 15 mins

The list of ingredients:

Meat Filling:

- Pinch of salt
- 1 pound lean, ground, or minced lamb
- 1/4 pint gravy
- Pinch of nutmeg
- Dash of pepper

Hot Water Pastry:

- 6 ounces lard
- 1 pound plain flour
- 2 egg yolks (beaten)
- Pinch of salt
- 3/4 cup water

Method:

Step 1

Preheat the main oven to 400 degrees F.

Step 2

First, make the filling. In a bowl, combine the lamb with the nutmeg, salt, and pepper. Add the gravy a little at a time as you do not want the mixture to be too loose. Set to one side.

Step 3

Start the pastry. Add the flour to a large bowl. Set aside for a moment.

Step 4

Add the salt, lard, and water to a saucepan and bring to a near boil. Take off the heat and pour over the flour in the bowl. Mix until combined with a wooden spoon. Flour your worktop and tip the dough onto it. Knead until you have a smooth dough. Set a ¼ of the pastry to one side.

Step 5

Split the remaining dough into 8 equal pieces and roll each into a ball. Roll each ball into a 6” wide, ¼” thick circle (these are the bases). Roll the remaining dough into 8, 3” circles (these will become the lids).

Step 6

Roll the filling into 8 equally-sized balls and place one on each base circle of dough.

Step 7

Gather the pastry up and around the filling ball, gently shaping into a pork pie shape. Keep stretching the pastry, gently, until it reaches about the meat by approximately ¾". Wet the pastry edges with a drop of water. Place a pastry lid on top of the filling ball. Press the high sides and lid together gently to seal.

Step 8

Wrap a strip of parchment around each pie and secure with string to help the pies keep their shape. Make a slit in the top of each pie and arrange on a baking tray.

Step 9

Brush each pie with beaten egg yolk. Chill the pies for half an hour.

Step 10

Place in the oven and bake for 45 minutes until browned and golden.

Step 11

Allow to cool a little before serving.

14. Chicken, Leek, Prune and Caerphilly Pie

Servings: 4-6

Prep Time: 15 mins

Cooking Time: 40 mins

Total Time: 55 mins

The list of ingredients:

- 1 tbsp. olive oil
- Salt
- Yolk of 1 medium egg
- Fresh parsley
- 1 tbsp. salted butter
- 18 ounces ready-rolled chilled puff pastry
- 3½ ounces prunes (halved)
- 1¾ ounces fresh tarragon (chopped)
- 7 ounces leeks, white parts only (sliced)
- 5 ounces Caerphilly cheese (crumbled)
- Pepper
- 4 boneless chicken thighs (chopped)
- 1 pint chicken stock
- 1 yellow onion (peeled, chopped)
- 7 ounces heavy cream
- 3 garlic cloves (peeled, sliced)
- 2 tbsp. flour
- 1 tbsp. double cream
- 2 tsp. English mustard
- 5 ounces white wine

Method:

Step 1

Preheat the main oven to 350 degrees F.

Step 2

In a pan melt the butter along with the oil and fry the chopped garlic and onions until they change color.

Step 3

Add the chicken, cook for another 5-6 minutes.

Step 4

Add the leeks followed by the flour, stirring until well incorporated.

Step 5

Gradually, add the white wine and stock until the sauce begins to thicken.

Step 6

Next, add the cream and English mustard and season.

Step 7

Take off the heat and add the prunes, Caerphilly cheese, tarragon, and parsley, stir to combine. Spoon into a pie dish.

Step 8

Combine the egg yolk and cream and lightly brush the mixture around the dish.

Step 9

Cover the filling with the pastry and trim the edges, before glazing with the remaining egg mixture.

Step 10

Make a few slits in the top of the pastry.

Step 11

Place in the oven and bake for just under half an hour. Allow to cool a little before serving.

15. Stargazey Pie

Servings: 6

Prep Time: 25 mins

Cooking Time: 50 mins

Total Time: 1 hour 15 mins

The list of ingredients:

- 1½ cups white breadcrumbs
- 5 ounces cider (local brew if possible)
- 1 egg (beaten, to glaze)
- 1/2 tsp. salt
- 1 onion (peeled, chopped)
- 3 eggs (hard-boiled, shelled, roughly chopped)
- 17½ ounces ready-made shortcrust pastry
- 3-4 tbsp parsley (chopped)
- 8 heads-on herring or mackerel (gutted, cleaned, boned)
- 1¾ ounce whole milk
- 1/2 tsp. pepper
- Juice and rind of 1 lemon
- 4 ounces streaky bacon (rind removed, chopped)

Method:

Step 1

Soak the breadcrumbs in milk until they are moist and combine with the freshly squeezed lemon juice and rind along with the half of the onion and the majority of the parsley and seasoning.

Step 2

Use the breadcrumb mixture to stuff the fish, sprinkling any leftover crumbs over the bottom of a circular, deep 9" pie dish.

Step 3

Arrange the herring with their heads pointing up towards the outer edge. Scatter in between the fish with the remaining onions, chopped parsley, chopped streaky bacon, and hardboiled eggs. Season generously and pour in the cider.

Step 4

Roll out the shortcrust pastry to fit the top of the pie dish, and use any scraps to make a pastry trim; this helps the lid to adhere to the top.

Step 5

Arrange the pastry on top and make a few slits on the top of the pie where the fish are and gently poke them through, so that they stand up.

Step 6

Gently press the edges together to seal, trim and lightly brush with beaten egg.

Step 7

Make a few more slits, but in the middle of the pie as this will help the steam escape.

Step 8

Bake in the oven at 400 degrees F for between 40-50 minutes, or until the pastry is golden.

Step 9

Sprinkle with the remaining parsley and serve.

16. Cheshire Pork Pie

Servings: 8

Prep Time: 20 mins

Cooking Time: 1 hour

Total Time: 1 hour 20 mins

The list of ingredients:

- Knob of butter

- Grated nutmeg

- 1 tsp. sugar

- 9¼ ounces white wine

- 1 small onion (peeled, chopped)

- 1 pound ready-made puff pastry (thawed)

- Salt and black pepper

- 3 Granny Smith apples (halved, cored, sliced)

- 1 medium egg (beaten)

- 2¼ pounds lean pork loin (diced, divided)

Method:

Step 1

Preheat the main oven to 360 degrees F. In a 9" pie dish, layer half of the pork, then all of the apples, sprinkle with sugar, then add the onions, and finish with a layer of pork. Season each layer with salt, pepper, and nutmeg.

Step 2

Pour the white wine over the mixture. Dot with butter.

Step 3

Roll out the ready-made puff pastry to fit the pie dish.

Step 4

Lightly brush the rim of the dish with beaten egg
and arrange the pastry on top.

Step 5

Gently but firmly press the dough down to form a
seal and make slits in the top of the pie, brush the
top with beaten egg.

Step 6

Bake in the oven for 60 minutes, or until the meat is
sufficiently cooked through. If after half an hour
you feel the pastry is browning too quickly, arrange
a piece of parchment paper on top.

17. Homity Pie

Servings: 6-8

Prep Time: 20mins

Cooking Time: 1 hour 15 mins

Total Time: 1hour 35 mins

The list of ingredients:

- 14 ounces shortcrust pastry

- 1 stalk of thyme

- 14 ounces potatoes (peeled)

- 2 tsp. mustard powder

- 2 garlic cloves

- Salt and black pepper

- 7 ounces cheddar cheese

- 2 ounces butter

- 4 yellow onions (peeled, finely sliced)

- 5 ounces double cream

Method:

Step 1

Preheat the main oven to 400 degrees F.

Step 2

Roll out the pastry and arrange in a 10" pie dish, line with parchment and add baking beans. Place in the oven and bake for 20 minutes. When baked, remove the beans.

Step 3

In a pan of boiling salted water, boil the potatoes until fork tender and chop into bite-sized cubes.

Step 4

In the meantime, in a pan melt the butter; add the thyme, onions, and garlic. Slowly cook until caramelized.

Step 5

Add in the potato and grated cheese, stir well then add the double cream and mustard powder. Season well.

Step 6

Pour the mixture into the pastry shell and cook for 15 minutes. Allow to cool a little before serving.

18. Corned Beef Pie

Servings: 3-4

Prep Time: 20 mins

Cooking Time: 1 hour

Total Time: 1 hour 20 mins

The list of ingredients:

Filling:

- 7 ounces frozen peas
- 1 medium onion (peeled, finely chopped)
- 3 splashes Worcestershire sauce
- 1 carrot (diced)
- 1 tbsp. vegetable oil
- 1 (12 ounce) can corned beef (diced)
- 2 tbsp. fresh parsley (chopped)
- 1 tbsp. tomato puree
- 1 cup vegetable stock
- 1 medium potato
- 1 tsp. sugar
- 1 stick celery (finely chopped)

Pastry:

- 3½ ounces lard
- 1¾ pounds plain flour
- Egg wash
- 3½ ounces margarine
- Cold water

Method:

Step 1

Heat a large pan and add the oil.

Step 2

Sauté the onion until softened. Add the carrots along with the celery and potatoes and cook for 5 minutes, until soft.

Step 3

Add the splashes of Worcestershire sauce, tomato puree, and sugar and fry for a couple of minutes. Pour in the stock and simmer.

Step 4

Add the diced corned beef together with the peas, adding additional stock if necessary to cover all of the ingredients.

Step 5

Continue simmering, while occasionally stirring until the carrots and potatoes are fork-tender, and the liquid is absorbed.

Step 6

Scatter with parsley and allow to cool a little.

Step 7

Next, prepare the pastry. Sieve the flour into a mixing bowl, add the margarine and lard and rub together to a breadcrumb-like consistency. Add enough water to combine.

Step 8

Cover the dough with plastic wrap and transfer to the refrigerator for a minimum of 20 minutes.

Step 9

Roll out ⅔ of the pastry and line a suitable pie dish.

Step 10

Roll out the remaining ⅓ of the pastry.

Step 11

Dampen the edges of the pastry around the rim of the pie dish.

Step 12

Add the filling to the pie and cover with the pastry lid and crimp to seal.

Step 13

Brush the pie all over with egg wash and prick in several places with a metal fork; this will allow the steam to escape.

Step 14

Bake in the oven at 360 degrees F for 35-40 minutes, or until the pastry is golden.

Step 15

Serve.

19. Game Pie

Servings: 6-8

Prep Time: 30 mins

Cooking Time: 2 hours 10 mins

Total Time: 2 hours 40 mins

The list of ingredients:

- 4¼ ounces smoked back bacon (diced)

- 1 clove garlic (peeled, crushed)
- Juice and zest of 1 orange
- 2 large red onions (peeled, diced)
- 1 medium egg (beaten)
- 4 bay leaves
- 2½ pounds ready-made shortcrust pastry
- 1 tbsp redcurrant jelly
- Salt pepper
- 2¼ pounds mixed game meat including venison, rabbit, pigeon, pheasant (bone, diced)
- 2 tbsp olive oil (divided)
- 1/3 cup port
- 1 ounce plain flour
- 4¼ ounces field mushrooms (sliced)
- 1¼ cups chicken stock

Method:

Step 1

Preheat the main oven to 375 degrees F.

Step 2

In a pan, heat 1 tbsp of oil, and in batches, brown the meat, and set to one side.

Step 3

Heat the remaining oil, and sweat off the red onions, until they are beginning to soften but not changing color. Add the garlic along with the mushrooms and smoked bacon and cook for between 2-3 minutes.

Step 4

Add the flour, and stir for 2 minutes. Season generously and stir in the bay leaves followed by the freshly squeezed orange juice, zest, jelly, chicken stock and port.

Step 5

Bring to the boil and add the meat, while gently simmering for 60 minutes, until the meat is fork tender. Taste and season. Set to one side to cool.

Step 6

Lightly flour the skillet, without greasing.

Step 7

Roll out the pastry base and gently press it into the skillet, allowing an overhang of approximately ½" and brush with beaten egg.

Step 8

Add the meat filling.

Step 9

Roll out the pastry for the lid.

Step 10

Place the lid on top of the filling and using a fork, gently press down to seal.

Step 11

Make a few slices in the top of the pie to allow the steam to escape and lightly brush all over, with beaten egg.

Step 12

Bake on the bottom shelf of the oven for half an hour.

Step 13

Transfer to the top shelf and bake for 30 minutes, or until the filling has reached an internal temperature of 150 degrees F and the pastry is golden.

Step 14

Cut and serve.

20. Country Style Tomato Pie

Servings: 4-6

Prep Time: 20 mins

Cooking Time: 40 mins

Total Time: 1 hour

The list of ingredients:

- 1 small bunch spring onions (thinly sliced)

- 1 cup full-fat mayo
- 1(9") deep ready-made pie shell (partially baked)
- Black pepper
- 3 large ripe tomatoes
- 1 tbsp. fresh basil (julienned)
- 1 cup sharp Cheddar cheese (grated)
- Sea salt

Method:

Step 1

Preheat the main oven to 350 degrees F.

Step 2

First, peel the tomatoes by cutting a small cross on the bottom of the tomato and then dipping into a pan of boiling water for 30-40 seconds. Remove from the water and immediately submerge into the iced water; this will enable you to peel the skin away.

Step 3

Slice the tomatoes into thick slices and arrange them, in layers, inside the pie shell. Sprinkle each of the layers with onions, basil, salt and black pepper.

Step 4

In a small bowl combine the mayo with the Cheddar
cheese and evenly spread over the tomatoes.

Step 5

Bake in the oven for between 30-40 minutes, until
the filling is gently browned.

Step 6

Remove from the oven and allow to rest for several
minutes before slicing

*You can julienne the basil by rolling into a cigar shape
and cutting crosswise.

21. Fish, Chip, and Mushy Pea Pie

Servings: 2

Prep Time: 25 mins

Cooking Time: 50 mins

Total Time: 1 hour 10 mins

The list of ingredients:

- Tartar sauce

- 1 large potato (peeled)

- 6 ounces garden peas

- 4¼ ounces ready-made shortcrust pastry

- Knob of butter

- 3½ ounces white fish fillet (cleaned)

Method:

Step 1

Preheat the main oven to 350 degrees F.

Step 2

Prepare the chips. Cut the potato into chunky chip shapes and in a pan of water, boil for 4-5 minutes.

Step 3

Transfer to a baking dish and place in the oven for half an hour, while regularly stirring.

Step 4

In the meantime, roll out the ready-made pastry and line a 4x5" pie tin. Using a fork. prick the bottom and inside edges of the pastry.

Step 5

Using parchment paper line the inside of the pastry, add baking beans, and blind bake for 15 minutes.

Step 6

Place the fish on a grill tray and place in the oven
for 15 minutes.

Step 7

In the meantime, make the mushy peas. In a pan of
boiling water, cook the peas, for 5 minutes. Drain.

Step 8

Return the peas to the pan; add a knob of butter and
mash.

Step 9

Remove the pie crust and the fish from the oven.
Taking out the baking beans.

Step 10

Layer the peas, fish, and tartar sauce in the pie. Top
off with the chipped potatoes.

Step 11

Return to the oven for 15 minutes, or until the chips
are crispy and the pastry golden.

Step 12

Serve.

22. Gala Pie

Servings: 8

Prep Time: 30 mins

Cooking Time: 1 hour 30 mins

Total Time: 2 hours

The list of ingredients:

Filling:

- 10½ ounces pork mince
- 3 tbsp. fresh parsley (chopped)
- 10½ ounces premium sausage meat
- 2 shallots (finely chopped)
- 4 medium eggs (hard-boiled, shelled)
- 5½ ounces cook ham hock (cut into ½" pieces)
- Salt and white pepper

Crust pastry:

- Water
- 1 medium egg (beaten)
- 1 pound plain flour + additional for dusting
- 2½ ounces unsalted butter (chilled, cut into ½" cubes)
- 3½ ounces lard
- 3½ ounces strong white flour
- 1/2 tsp. salt

Method:

Step 1

Preheat the main oven to 400 degrees F. Lightly grease a loaf tin of approximately 4x8". Cut one long strip of parchment paper and arrange it in the tin, so that there is an overhang.

Step 2

Prepare the filling. Add the sausage meat, pork mince, ham hock, shallots, parsley, and seasoning into a mixing bowl. Using clean hands mix to incorporate.

Step 3

Transfer the mixture to the refrigerator while you prepare the pastry.

Step 4

In a bowl, combine the flours with the butter and using clean fingertips, lightly rub.

Step 5

In a small pan, heat 7 ounces of water, ½ tsp salt, and the lard until just boiling.

Step 6

Pour the mixture onto the flour and combine, using a spoon. Once the mixture is sufficiently cool to handle, transfer to a lightly floured worktop and knead into smooth dough.

Step 7

Workings as speedily as possible, roll out ⅔ of the dough. Transfer it to the prepared tin, allowing any excess to hang over the edges of the tin.

Step 8

Press approximately half of the meat filling into the pastry-lined loaf tin.

Step 9

Slice the top and bottom off each of the hard-boiled eggs, and arrange them, lengthways down the center of the piece. Add the remainder of the meat filling and gently pat it down.

Step 10

Make a pie lid, by rolling out the remaining pastry and laying it on top of the filling.

Step 11

Pinch the edges of the pastry together to form a seal and neatly trim the edges.

Step 12

Make 3 slits in the top of the pie, and brush with beaten egg yolk.

Step 13

Bake in the preheated oven for half an hour, before reducing the heat to 360 degrees F. Bake for another 60 minutes.

Step 14

Allow to cool in the tin.

Step 15

When you are ready to remove the pie from the tin, turn the loaf tin on its side and carefully slide it out, using the parchment paper.

23. Coronation Chicken Pie

Servings: 4-6

Prep Time: 20 mins

Cooking Time: 1 hour

Total Time: 1 hour 20 mins

The list of ingredients:

- 2 tbsp. raisins

- Salt and pepper

- 1 tbsp. olive oil

- 3/4 ounce malt vinegar

- 4 organic chicken breasts (diced)

- 3½ ounces ghee (melted)

- 1 ounce flour

- 1½ ounces flaked almonds

- 4 garlic cloves (peeled, grated)

- 12 ounces chicken stock

- 2 onions (peeled, diced)

- 1 tbsp. cilantro (chopped, to garnish)

- Large knob of butter

- 1 (9½ ounce) package ready-made filo pastry sheets

- 2 tbsp. ground almonds

- 2 tbsp mild curry powder

Method:

Step 1

Preheat the main oven to 380 degrees F.

Step 2

In a large pan, melt the oil along with the butter over moderate heat. Add the onions followed by the garlic and cook until softened.

Step 3

Add the flour together with the curry powder and cook for a couple of minutes.

Step 4

A little a time whisk in the stock and while continually stirring, simmer, until the mixture thickens.

Step 5

Add the chicken and poach until cooked through, this will take around 10 minutes.

Step 6

Stir in the raisins, almonds and malt vinegar. Season and pour into a shallow dish to cool.

Step 7

Lightly brush 4 of the pastry sheets with ghee and arrange in the base of a 9" pie tin, allowing any excess pastry to hang over the rim of the dish.

Step 8

Place the cooled filling into the pie tin, folding the overhanging pastry over the fillings.

Step 9

Brush the remaining pastry sheets with ghee and lay them on top, ensuring that the whole pie is sufficiently covered.

Step 10

Bake in the preheated oven for 15 minutes.

Step 11

Remove from the oven and garnish with almonds.

Step 12

Place the pie back in the oven for another 15 minutes, until crispy and gently browned.

Step 13

Remove and garnish with cilantro.

Step 14

Serve.

24. Katt Pie

Servings: 8-10

Prep Time: 20 mins

Cooking Time: 40 mins

Total Time: 1 hour

The list of ingredients:

- 7 ounces currants

- Salt and black pepper

- 6 ounce brown sugar

- 1 pound ready-made shortcrust pastry block

- 1 medium egg (beaten, to glaze)

- Rind of 1 large lemon

- 1 pound minced lamb

- 2-3 sprigs thyme

Method:

Step 1

Roll out half of the shortcrust pastry and line a 10"
pie dish.

Step 2

Add in layers, the lamb, currants, followed by the
sugar and lemon rind.

Step 3

Scatter with thyme, salt, and pepper.

Step 4

Roll out the remaining shortcrust pastry to make a
pie lid, arrange over the top of the filling, pinching
the edges together to seal. Trim away excess dough
and make a few slits on the top of the pie.

Step 5

Lightly brush with beaten eggs to glaze and bake in
the oven set at 400 degrees F, for approximately 35
minutes, until golden brown.

25. Smoked Fish Pie in Shortcrust Pastry

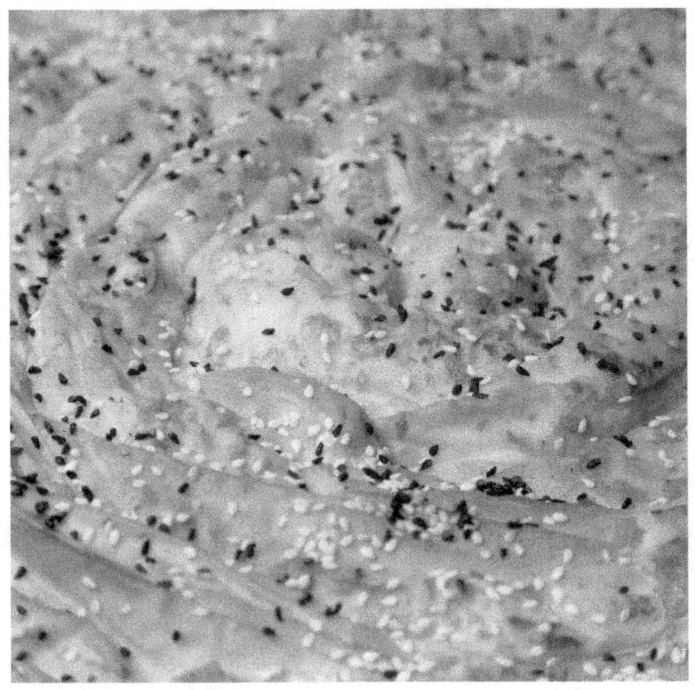

Servings: 4 individual pies

Prep Time: 15 mins

Cooking Time: 30 mins

Total Time: 1 hour

The list of ingredients:

- 1/2 cup white wine
- 3 ounces watercress (remove stalks)
- 1 (13 ounces) block ready-made shortcrust pastry
- 8 ounces broccoli florets (blanched, drained, cooled)
- Sesame seeds
- 5¼ ounces crème fraiche
- 8 ounces smoked salmon fillets
- Butter
- 13 ounces smoked haddock (undyed)

Method:

Step 1

Place the salmon and haddock fillets on a shallow, lightly buttered dish, add the white wine and cover the dish with plastic wrap. Microwave on a high setting for between 3-4 minutes. The fish is sufficiently cooked when it flakes easily with a fork and is opaque.

Step 2

Set to one side to cool.

Step 3

As soon as the salmon and haddock are cooled, drain and retain the stock.

Step 4

Remove any skin and using a fork, flake the fish into large pieces and evenly divide between 4 dishes together with the broccoli.

Step 5

Using food blender, process the watercress along with the crème fraiche and add the fish stock.

Step 6

Pour the mixture over the fish, filling each of the 4 dishes.

Step 7

Roll the pastry out and use it to cover each of the 4 pie dishes, having first formed a pastry rim around the top edge, this will make sure that the lid doesn't collapse into the pie filling.

Step 8

Brush the top of each pie with beaten egg and scatter with sesame seeds.

Step 9

Transfer the pies to oven and bake for approximately 20 minutes at 400 degrees F, until golden.

Sweet

26. Nutmeg Spiced Custard Tarts

Servings: 8

Prep Time: 30 mins

Cooking Time: 1 hour 15 mins

Total Time: 6 hours 45 mins

The list of ingredients:

Pastry:

- 1 medium egg

- 8 tbsp unsalted butter (at room temperature)

- 2½ cups plain flour

- 1/2 cup granulated sugar

- 1/4 tsp. kosher salt

Filling:

- 2/3 cup whole milk

- Yolks of 4 medium eggs

- 1/2 cup light brown sugar

- 2⅔ cup heavy cream

- Scrapings of ½ a vanilla bean

- 2 medium eggs

- 2 tsp. fresh nutmeg (grated)

Method:

Step 1

Using a hand mixer, beat together the butter and sugar in a bowl for 1-2 minutes.

Step 2

Add an egg and beat again. Then add the salt and
flour, mix for a final couple of minutes until you
have a crumbly dough. Split the dough into 4 equal
pieces.

Step 3

Flour your worktop. Roll each piece of dough into
an 1/8 " thick disk.

Step 4

Take 4 (6 ounce) mini tart tins. Arrange a dough
disk in each one and trim away any excess dough.

Step 5

Prick the base of each dough several times with a
fork. Chill for an hour.

Step 6

Preheat the main oven to 375 degrees F.

Step 7

Line each dough shell with a sheet of parchment
and fill with rice.

Step 8

Place the tart tins in the oven and bake for 15
minutes. Discard the rice and parchment, bake for
another 12-14 minutes. Transfer the pastry shells to
wire racks to completely cool.

Step 9

Turn the oven temperature down to 300 degrees F.

Step 10

Make the egg custard filling. In a saucepan over moderately high heat, bring to a simmer the milk, cream, vanilla bean scrapings, and nutmeg. When simmering, take off the heat.

Step 11

In a mixing bowl, whisk together the brown sugar, whole eggs, and egg yolks. Add the hot cream mixture to the eggs a little a time, while whisking, until combined.

Step 12

Arrange the tart shells on a baking sheet. Pour the custard filling equally into the tart shells and place on a rack in the middle of the oven. Bake for just over half an hour. Allow to completely cool, then chill for 3-4 hours before serving.

Step 13

When ready to serve, allow the tarts to come to room temperature.

27. Lemon Meringue Pie

Servings: 8

Prep Time: 20 mins

Cooking Time: 20 mins

Total Time: 40 mins

The list of ingredients:

Lemon Filling:

- Pinch kosher salt
- 1½ cups water
- 2 tbsp. salted butter
- Yolks of 3 medium eggs (beaten)
- 6 tbsp. cornstarch
- 1½ cups granulated sugar
- Fresh juice of 3 medium lemons
- 1 (9") baked pie shell
- 2 tsp. lemon peel (grated)

Meringue Topping:

- 1/4 tsp. cream of tartar
- Whites of 3 medium eggs (at room temperature)
- 6 tbsp granulated sugar
- 1/2 tsp. vanilla essence

Method:

Step 1

Preheat the main oven to 350 degrees F.

Step 2

Over moderately high heat, add the cornstarch, salt, and sugar in a saucepan. Whisk in the water until combined and thick. Turn the heat down to moderate and cook for another couple of minutes.

Step 3

Add the egg yolks to a small bowl, ladle in a cup of the cornstarch mixture and whisk until combined. Add the mixture to the saucepan.

Step 4

Stirring continually, bring the mixture to a boil for 2 minutes. Take off the heat and whisk in the lemon peel, juice, and butter. Pour into the pastry shell.

Step 5

Make the meringue. Whip up egg whites, vanilla, and cream of tartar until the mixture can hold stiff peaks. With the electric whisk running, add the sugar a little at a time until the mixture can hold stiff peaks.

Step 6

Dollop on top of the lemon filling right to the edges. Make sure there are no gaps at the edges.

Step 7

Place in the oven and bake for just under 15 minutes. Allow to completely cool before serving.

28. Plum, Apple, and Sloe Gin Pie

Servings: 6-8

Prep Time: 30 mins

Cooking Time: 1 hour

Total Time: 1 hour 30 mins

The list of ingredients:

- Heavy cream (for serving)

- White of 1 medium egg (beaten until frothy)

- 8 ripe plums (stoned, finely chopped)

- 2 tbsp corn flour

- 1 (13¼ ounce) package prepared sweet shortcrust pastry (chilled)

- 1/2 cup sloe gin

- 1/2 cup + 2 tsp. fine sugar

- 1 tbsp. white sugar

- 1/4 tsp. cinnamon

- 4 large Bramley apples (cored, peeled, finely chopped)

Method:

Step 1

In a wide saucepan over moderate heat, add the plums, apples, cornflour, sugar, and cinnamon. Cook for 5-6 minutes until slightly softened and saucy. Take off the heat and pour in the gin. Stir well and set to one side to cool.

Step 2

Preheat the main oven to 375 degrees F.

Step 3

Pour the cooled filling into an 8" deep-crust pie dish. Brush the edges of the dish with beaten egg white.

Step 4

Dust the work surface. Place the disk of rolled-out dough on top of the pie plate so that it is 0.2" thick. Trim any extra, then gently push to help the dish stay.

Step 5

Brush the top of the pie pastry with the remaining egg white and sprinkle with sugar.

Step 6

Pop in the oven and bake for just over 40 minutes.

Step 7

Allow to cool a little before serving with heavy cream.

*Can be found in specialty liquor stores.

29. Banoffee Pie

Servings: 8

Prep Time: 15 mins

Cooking Time: N/A

Total Time: 35 mins

The list of ingredients:

- 3 ripe, large bananas (peeled, sliced ¼" thick)

- 2 cups canned caramel/dulce de leche

- 1 tbsp. light brown sugar

- 1 (9") baked pie shell

- 1½ cups heavy whipping cream (chilled)

Method:

Step 1

Pour the toffee into the pie shell and smooth the surface until it is sitting in an even layer. Chill for 20 minutes.

Step 2

Arrange the sliced bananas in a neat, even layer on top of the toffee.

Step 3

Whip up the cream and sugar using an electric whisk until it can hold stiff peaks.

Step 4

Dollop on top of the pie in a cloud and serve!

30. Manchester Tart

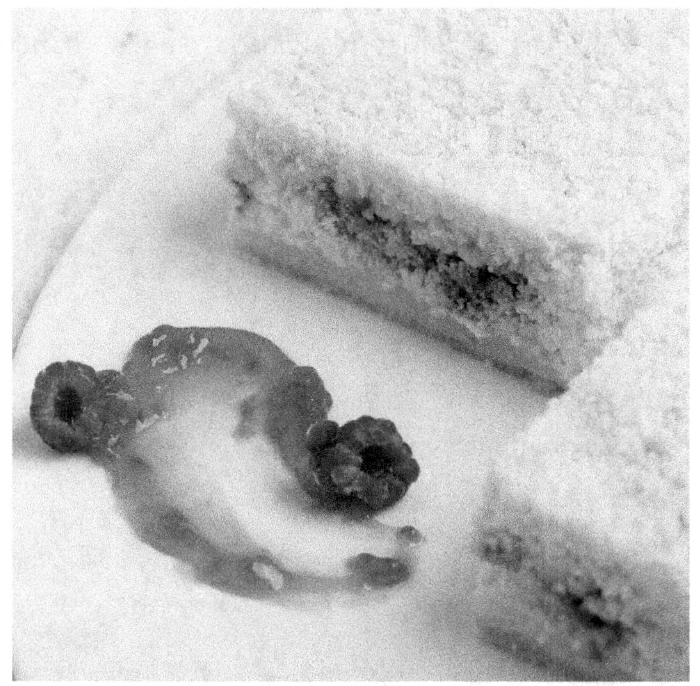

Servings: 8

Prep Time: 20 mins

Cooking Time: 30 mins

Total Time: 2 hours 30mins

The list of ingredients:

- 1 (11 ounce) sheet readymade chilled shortcrust pastry
- 3½ tbsp. organic raspberry jam
- 2 cups whole milk
- 5 tbsp. desiccated coconut
- 2 tbsp. fine sugar
- 3 tbsp custard powder
- 1 tsp. vanilla essence

Methods

Step 1

Preheat the main oven to 400 degrees F.

Step 2

Roll out the pastry and arrange in a 9" pie dish. Prick the base several times with a fork then line with a sheet of parchment. Pour rice on top of the parchment. Pop in the oven and bake for 20 minutes. Discard the rice and parchment, set to one side and allow the crust to cool.

Step 3

In a saucepan over moderate heat, add the custard powder, milk, vanilla, and sugar. Stir while cooking

until the mixture is smooth and thick. Take off the
heat and allow to completely cool.

Step 4

In the base of the pastry shell, spread the jam in an
even layer. Pour over the custard and scatter with
the coconut.

Step 5

Chill for 1-2 hours before serving.

31. Mini Jam Jewel Tarts

Servings: 24 (2 tarts per serving)

Prep Time: 20 mins

Cooking Time: 15 mins

Total Time: 1 hour 5 mins

The list of ingredients:

Pastry:

- 1 medium egg
- 1/2 cup salted butter (at room temperature)
- 1½ cups all-purpose flour
- 1/4 cup granulated sugar

Filling:

- 1/4 cup organic apricot jam
- 1/4 cup organic blackberry jam
- 1/4 cup organic cherry jam

Method:

Step 1

Using an electric mixer, beat together the butter and sugar until creamy.

Step 2

Beat in the egg.

Step 3

With the mixer running, beat in the flour, a little at a time, until you have a combined dough.

Step 4

Split the dough into 2 equal pieces and cover with plastic wrap, chill for half an hour.

Step 5

Preheat the main oven to 375 degrees F.

Step 6

Flour your worktop and roll each piece of dough out into a thin 1/10"sheet.

Step 7

Use a 2¼" cookie cutter to cut circles out of the dough. Arrange each circle in the individual holes of mini-tart tins.

Step 8

Fill a third of the pastry shells with cherry jam, another third with apricot jam, and the remaining third with blackberry jam.

Step 9

Place in the oven and bake for 10-12 minutes until golden. Allow to cool completely before serving.

32. Apple and Blackberry Pie

Servings: 8

Prep Time: 25 mins

Cooking Time: 1 hour

Total Time: 2 hours 25 mins

The list of ingredients:

Pastry:

- 1 cup salted butter (chilled, cubed)
- 1/2 tsp. kosher salt
- 1/3-2/3 cup ice-cold water
- 2½ cups all-purpose flour

Filling:

- Whole milk
- 1½ cups frozen blackberries
- 2 tbsp. all-purpose flour
- 2 pounds Granny Smith apples (cored, peeled, quarters, sliced ¼" thick)
- Sweetened whip cream (for serving)
- 1/3 cup + 2 tsp granulated sugar

Method:

Step 1

Sift together the salt and flour into a bowl.

Step 2

Using two knives, cut in the chilled butter until you have a crumbly textured mixture.

Step 3

While tossing with a metal fork, splash in a little water at a time until your dough is smooth that it holds together when pressed.

Step 4

Divide the dough into two balls and roll each into a disk shape. Cover with plastic wrap and chill for an hour.

Step 5

Flour your worktop. Roll out one piece of chilled dough into a (⅛") disk. Arrange in a (9") pie dish. Trim any excess and set to one side while you prepare the filling.

Step 6

Preheat the main oven to 375 degrees F.

Step 7

In a large bowl, combine the blackberries, apples, ⅓ cup granulated sugar, and flour. Tip into the pie dish.

Step 8

Roll out the second piece of dough, as before, and place over the filling. Trim any excess, press the top and bottom doughs together. Make several small slits in the top of the pie.

Step 9

Brush the top of the pie with milk and sprinkle with the remaining granulated sugar.

Step 10

Place in the oven and bake for just under an hour.

Step 11

Allow to cool to warm before serving with whip cream.

33. Mince Pie

Servings: 6-8

Prep Time: 15 mins

Cooking Time: 1 hour

Total Time: 2 hours

The list of ingredients:

Pie crust:

- 1/3 cup shortening
- 1/2 tsp. kosher salt
- 4-5 tbsp. ice-cold water
- 1¼ cups all-purpose flour

Filling:

- 1/4 cup salted butter (melted)
- Pinch kosher salt
- 1 cup jarred mincemeat
- 2 tbsp all-purpose flour
- 1/2 cup walnuts (chopped)
- 1 cup granulated sugar
- 3 medium eggs (lightly beaten)

Method:

Step 1

Preheat the main oven to 450 degrees F.

Step 2

Sift together the salt and flour into a bowl.

Step 3

Use two knives to cut in the shortening until you have a mixture with a crumbly texture.

Step 4

Roll out the dough into an even sheet and arrange in a 9" pie dish, flute the edges of the pastry.

Step 5

Line with two sheets of aluminum foil and pop in the oven for 5 minutes, discard the foil and bake for another 5 minutes. Set to one side to cool. Turn the oven temperature down to 350 degrees F.

Step 6

Combine the flour, salt, and sugar in a bowl and then mix in the melted butter, beaten eggs, chopped walnuts, and mincemeat. Spoon into the pie crust and bake in the oven for just over 40 minutes.

Step 7

Allow to cool completely before serving.

*Can be found in most delicatessens and supermarket baking sections.

34. Gypsy Tart

Servings: 8

Prep Time: 20 mins

Cooking Time: 30 mins

Total Time: 2 hours 50 mins

The list of ingredients:

- 1 (14½ ounce) can evaporated milk

- 1 (9") baked shortcrust pastry shell
- 12½ ounces muscovado sugar

Method:

Step 1

Preheat the main oven to 400 degrees F.

Step 2

Whisk together the sugar and milk while using an electric mixer for 10-12 minutes until frothy.

Step 3

Pour the mixture into the pastry shell.

Step 4

Pop in the oven and bake for 20-30 minutes, the filling should be set and only a little wobbly right in the middle.

Step 5

Allow to completely cool then chill for at least 2 hours before serving.

35. Bakewell Tart

Servings: 8-10

Prep Time: 20 mins

Cooking Time: 1 hour 25 mins

Total Time: 2 hours 30 mins

The list of ingredients:

Pastry Crust:

- 1¼ cups all-purpose flour
- 1/2 tsp. kosher salt
- 3 tbsp ice cold water
- 1/2 tsp. granulated sugar
- 6 tbsp unsalted butter (chilled, cubed)

Filling:

- 1 cup salted, roasted, almonds (finely ground)
- Whites of 3 large eggs
- Scrapings of 1/2 a vanilla bean
- Pinch kosher salt
- Yolks of 4 large eggs
- 3/4 cup organic raspberry preserves
- 1/2 cup unsalted butter (melted, cool)
- 1/4 tsp. almond essence
- 1/2 cup granulated sugar

Method:

Step 1

In a food processor, add the salt, sugar, and flour. Blitz for 5-6 seconds to combine. Add the butter, pulse until you have a coarse meal. Then add the water and blend until you have a dough that comes together. Add more water if it is too dry.

Step 2

Transfer the dough to a worktop and roughly form into a disk. Cover with plastic kitchen wrap and chill for an hour.

Step 3

Preheat the main oven to 375 degrees F.

Step 4

Roll out the cold dough into a 12" circle on a floured surface and place it in a 9" pie dish with a detachable bottom. Trim away all but 12" of the excess, fold it over to make a "lip," and then freeze for 10 minutes.

Step 5

Line the frozen crust with aluminum foil and fill with rice. Pop in the oven and bake for 25 minutes. Discard the foil and rice, bake for another 12-14 minutes. Allow to cool.

Step 6

Turn the oven temperature to 350 degrees F.

Step 7

Spread the raspberry preserves in an even layer in the base of the cooled crust.

Step 8

Add the sugar and vanilla bean scrapings to a bowl. Combine using a fork.

Step 9

Beat in the egg whites, yolks, melted butter, almond essence, and kosher salt. When combined, mix in the finely ground almonds.

Step 10

Spoon the filling into the pie crust.

Step 11

Place in the oven and bake for just over half an hour.

Step 12

Allow to cool to warm/room temperature before slicing and serving.

36. Bilberry Lattice Pie

Servings: 8

Prep Time: 15 mins

Cooking Time: 45 mins

Total Time: 1 hour 15 mins

The list of ingredients:

- Flour (for worktop)

- 3/4 cup heavy cream

- Fresh juice of 1/2 a medium lemon

- 9 ounces ready-rolled sweet shortcrust pastry

- 2 tbsp. cornflour

- 1 egg (lightly beaten)

- 17½ ounces fresh bilberries

- 1 tbsp. granulated sugar

- 1/3 cup fine sugar

Method:

Step 1

Add the bilberries, sugar, cornflour, and lemon juice to a large bowl. Toss to combine and set to one side for 15 minutes.

Step 2

Preheat the main oven to 375 degrees F.

Step 3

Sprinkle your worktop with flour and roll out the pastry into a thin sheet. Arrange the pastry in a 9" pie dish. Trim away the excess (there should be plenty).

Step 4

Roll out the trimmed pastry into an even, thin sheet and slice into equal-sized strips. Set to one side for a moment.

Step 5

Tip the bilberry mixture into the pie dish.

Step 6

Arrange the pastry strips on top of the filling in a simple lattice design. Press down gently on all seams to seal.

Step 7

Brush the exposed pastry with beaten egg and sprinkle with sugar.

Step 8

Pop in the oven and bake for just over 45 minutes until bubbly.

Step 9

Allow to cool to warm before serving with cream.

37. Maids of Honour Pies

Servings: 24

Prep Time: 25 mins

Cooking Time: 25 mins

Total Time: 50 mins

The list of ingredients:

Filling:

- Zest of 2 medium lemons (finely grated)
- 1 cup ricotta cheese
- Juice of 1 medium lemon
- Pinch kosher salt
- 1/3 cup white sugar
- 3 tbsp organic lemon curd
- 3 medium eggs
- 1/3 cup finely ground almonds

Pastry:

- Powdered sugar
- 16 ounces readymade chilled puff pastry

Method:

Step 1

Preheat the main oven to 400 degrees F.

Step 2

In a mixing bowl, combine the ricotta cheese, sugar, lemon zest, lemon juice, ground almonds, kosher salt, and eggs until smooth. Set to one side.

Step 3

Sprinkle your worktop with flour and roll the puff pastry into a ⅛" thick sheet. Use a 3" fluted cookie cutter to cut 24 circles from the dough.

Step 4

Take 2 (12-hole) muffin tins. Arrange a pastry disk in each hole. Spoon a teaspoon of lemon curd into every pastry, followed by a teaspoon of the ricotta mixture.

Step 5

Pop in the oven and bake for just over 20 minutes until risen and golden.

Step 6

Allow to completely cool before dusting with powdered sugar and serving.